The Power of 1°

Participant's Guide

Essential One-Year Devotional Series for Worship Ministries

MARK MATTINGLY

Worship team members should use this Participant's Guide, while leaders use:

"The Power of 1° - Leader's Guide"

Acknowledgments

"*The Power of 1°*" was birthed from a culmination of truths about God, scripture and life that have been poured into me by more people than I can possibly acknowledge. From pastors, mentors, Bible Study leaders, Sunday School teachers, family, friends, colleagues and more, they have all impacted this book in more ways than I can imagine.

With this in mind, there are some very special people I would like to thank. First, I want to thank my wife, Tonya. I don't know how to even begin thanking you for your seemingly never-ending love, support and patience with me. I love you. For our four sons: Tyler, Blake, Hudson and Jack. For helping me laugh more than I deserve and love deeper than I thought possible. It is a blessing to be a father to such incredible young men. For my parents raising me in a Godly home. Thanks to my great graphics artist, James Tyree. Also, for all of the family members, friends, editors and others that contributed to this book coming to fruition. Most importantly, I want to thank my Lord for being my Hope, my Salvation and my God. You are everything to me.

Dedication

To my beautiful wife, Tonya,
and our four sons: Tyler, Blake, Hudson and Jack

Shaded Edition: The words of Jesus Christ
can be found *shaded* throughout the scripture verses.

First Printing 2017
Printed in the United States of America

Cover Design: James Tyree

ISBN 978-0-9990080-1-0

For more information, contact us at:
PowerOfOneDegree@gmail.com

Table of Contents

True Story

Years ago, an eight-year-old boy attended an evening worship service at a church in the Midwest. While voices sang and instruments played, God began to speak to the young lad. As the service ended and the family headed home, the young boy was heavy-hearted. From the back seat of the car, the son leaned forward and whispered to his dad that he needed to talk with him. When they got home, the son told his father he felt God was speaking to him. There was something he was supposed to do, but the son didn't quite understand it all. The father went with the son to his room and shared the Good News of the Gospel with him. The son prayed to accept Jesus Christ as his Lord and Savior on the edge of his bed that night.

Do you know who the son was? That was me. An average little boy in a typical, Midwestern church surrendered his life to Jesus through a seemingly ordinary worship service. The people leading worship that evening were unaware that God had used them to point me to Christ. Through their service and obedience, my life was changed forever. What the worship leader did that night impacted me for eternity. Likewise, what you do each and every week as a worship leader can also be used by God to impact souls for eternity.

Be encouraged: What you do as a worship leader each week matters. You never know what extraordinary activities God is doing in what appears to be an ordinary worship service. Be faithful in pointing people to Christ in every worship service you lead. Be prayed up and expect God to do amazing things each week. Only He can do the extraordinary with the ordinary...

Introduction

As a member of your worship ministry team, you pour your heart into preparing for each corporate gathering to make it the best worship experience possible. You attend rehearsals, practice songs, and work out vocal and instrumental parts. You may also work on perfecting instrumental riffs, blending the vocals and selecting just the right sounds. This is, of course, on top of being a part of refining the overall rhythms, dynamics, melodies, harmonies, style and tempo among many other musical factors. Consequently, music and music-related issues can easily become our dominant focus and consume our thoughts and attention.

With all this in mind, is there a dedicated time during rehearsals where you and your team members grow deeper in your spiritual walk? Are you participating in a dynamic devotional each week with your team members that is geared towards worship and intended to help you grow in your relationship with Christ as a worshipper? This is what "The Power of 1°" is specifically designed to do.

"The Power of 1°" seeks to align worship leaders and team members with what God intended worship to be about: *Him*. To become better leaders of worship, it is imperative we get to know God, the object of our worship, better. By using "The Power of 1°" over the next 52 weeks, you and your team members will embark on an adventure to learn more about

God and worship. You will be challenged through these five-minute weekly devotionals to see worship from God's perspective and align your heart with His. While you follow along in "The Power of 1° - Participant's Guide", your leader will guide you by using "The Power of 1° - Leader's Guide".

I trust you will grow deeper in love with Jesus, more clearly understand your role as a worshipper and become more effective in leading others into the presence of God. It is my privilege to join you as you travel the road of this new spiritual journey. It is my prayer that these devotionals will help propel you closer to Him.

Proverbs 4:27

27 Do not swerve to the right or to the left; turn your foot away from evil.

Notes and Thoughts:

Question(s) of the Week: Are you seeking God and His will for your life, or your own?

Answer:

The Power of 1°

Eliashib and the Sheep Gate

Nehemiah 3:1

1 Then Eliashib the high priest rose up with his brothers the priests, and they built the Sheep Gate. They consecrated it and set its doors. They consecrated it as far as the Tower of the Hundred, as far as the Tower of Hananel.

Notes and Thoughts:

Question(s) of the Week: Is knowing God and worshipping Him your top priority?

Answer:

_____ **The Power of 1°**

James 4:6

6 But he gives more grace. Therefore it says, "God opposes the proud, but gives grace to the humble."

Notes and Thoughts:

Question(s) of the Week: Have the skills and talents God has entrusted to you turned into pride or arrogance in any way?

Answer:

The Power of 1°

Matthew 18:15-17

15 "If your brother sins against you, go and tell him his fault, between you and him alone. If he listens to you, you have gained your brother.

16 But if he does not listen, take one or two others along with you, that every charge may be established by the evidence of two or three witnesses.

17 If he refuses to listen to them, tell it to the church. And if he refuses to listen even to the church, let him be to you as a Gentile and a tax collector."

Notes and Thoughts:

Question(s) of the Week: Is there <u>any</u> believer you currently have an unresolved conflict with? What steps will you take to resolve the situation and get into a right relationship with both them and God?

Answer:

The Power of 1°

Matthew 5:43-47

43 *"You have heard that it was said, 'You shall love your neighbor and hate your enemy.'*

44 *But I say to you, Love your enemies and pray for those who persecute you,*

45 *so that you may be sons of your Father who is in heaven. For he makes his sun rise on the evil and on the good, and sends rain on the just and on the unjust.*

46 *For if you love those who love you, what reward do you have? Do not even the tax collectors do the same?*

47 *And if you greet only your brothers, what more are you doing than others? Do not even the Gentiles do the same?"*

Notes and Thoughts:

Question(s) of the Week: Who is God bringing to your mind that you need to love and/or forgive?

Answer:

The Power of 1°

1 John 2:3

3 And by this we know that we have come to know him, if we keep his commandments.

Notes and Thoughts:

Question(s) of the Week: Would Christians close to you say there is significant evidence to indicate you are a believer? Why or why not?

Answer:

The Power of 1°

Deuteronomy 5:7

7 You shall have no other gods before me.

Notes and Thoughts:

Question(s) of the Week: How are you currently "worshipping the conduit" of worship, rather than worshipping God?

Answer:

The Power of 1°

Unacceptable Worship

Genesis 4:1-7

1 Now Adam knew Eve his wife, and she conceived and bore Cain, saying, "I have gotten a man with the help of the LORD."

2 And again, she bore his brother Abel. Now Abel was a keeper of sheep, and Cain a worker of the ground.

3 In the course of time Cain brought to the LORD an offering of the fruit of the ground,

4 and Abel also brought of the firstborn of his flock and of their fat portions. And the LORD had regard for Abel and his offering,

5 but for Cain and his offering he had no regard. So Cain was very angry, and his face fell.

6 The LORD said to Cain, "Why are you angry, and why has your face fallen?

7 If you do well, will you not be accepted? And if you do not do well, sin is crouching at the door. Its desire is contrary to you, but you must rule over it."

Question(s) of the Week: *Is your personal worship led by faith or out of obligation each week?*

Answer:

The Power of 1°

The Humble Stutterer

Read: Numbers 12:1-10a

Numbers 12:1-10a

1 Miriam and Aaron spoke against Moses because of the Cushite woman whom he had married, for he had married a Cushite woman.

2 And they said, "Has the Lord indeed spoken only through Moses? Has he not spoken through us also?" And the Lord heard it.

3 Now the man Moses was very meek, more than all people who were on the face of the earth.

4 And suddenly the Lord said to Moses and to Aaron and Miriam, "Come out, you three, to the tent of meeting." And the three of them came out.

5 And the Lord came down in a pillar of cloud and stood at the entrance of the tent and called Aaron and Miriam, and they both came forward.

6 And he said, "Hear my words: If there is a prophet among you, I the Lord make myself known to him in a vision; I speak with him in a dream.

7 Not so with my servant Moses. He is faithful in all my house.

8 With him I speak mouth to mouth, clearly, and not in riddles, and he beholds the form of the Lord. Why then were you not afraid to speak against my servant Moses?"

9 And the anger of the Lord was kindled against them, and he departed.

10a When the cloud removed from over the tent, behold, Miriam was leprous, like snow.

Notes and Thoughts:

Question(s) of the Week: *Would your closest friends describe you as "humble"? If not, what evidence is there that gives them this impression?*

Answer:

The Power of 1°

Ephesians 5:1

1 Therefore be imitators of God, as beloved children.

Notes and Thoughts:

Question(s) of the Week: What evidence is there in your life that God is truly your role model? Are you effectively imitating Him?

Answer:

The Power of 1°

Matthew 27:50-54

50 And Jesus cried out again with a loud voice and yielded up his spirit.

51 And behold, the curtain of the temple was torn in two, from top to bottom. And the earth shook, and the rocks were split.

52 The tombs also were opened. And many bodies of the saints who had fallen asleep were raised,

53 and coming out of the tombs after his resurrection they went into the holy city and appeared to many.

54 When the centurion and those who were with him, keeping watch over Jesus, saw the earthquake and what took place, they were filled with awe and said, "Truly this was the Son of God!"

Notes and Thoughts:

Question(s) of the Week: Do you try to lead others into God's presence through your own strength or through His?

Answer:

_____ *The Power of 1°*

Daniel 3 (Portions)

1 *King Nebuchadnezzar made an image of gold, whose height was sixty cubits and its breadth six cubits. He set it up on the plain of Dura, in the province of Babylon.*

4 *And the herald proclaimed aloud, "You are commanded, O peoples, nations, and languages,*
5 *that when you hear the sound of the horn, pipe, lyre, trigon, harp, bagpipe, and every kind of music, you are to fall down and worship the golden image that King Nebuchadnezzar has set up.*
6 *And whoever does not fall down and worship shall immediately be cast into a burning fiery furnace."*

13 *Then Nebuchadnezzar in furious rage commanded that Shadrach, Meshach, and Abednego be brought. So they brought these men before the king.*
14 *Nebuchadnezzar answered and said to them, "Is it true, O Shadrach, Meshach, and Abednego, that you do not serve my gods or worship the golden image that I have set up?*
15 *Now if you are ready when you hear the sound of the horn, pipe, lyre, trigon, harp, bagpipe, and every kind of music, to fall down and worship the image that I have made, well and good. But if you do not worship, you shall immediately be cast into a burning fiery furnace. And who is the god who will deliver you out of my hands?"*

16 Shadrach, Meshach, and Abednego answered and said to the king, "O Nebuchadnezzar, we have no need to answer you in this matter.

17 If this be so, our God whom we serve is able to deliver us from the burning fiery furnace, and he will deliver us out of your hand, O king.

18 But if not, be it known to you, O king, that we will not serve your gods or worship the golden image that you have set up."

Notes and Thoughts:

Question(s) of the Week: As worshippers, are you living now with a constant and unwavering faith?

Answer:

The Power of 1°

Mark 14:26

26 And when they had sung a hymn, they went out to the Mount of Olives.

Notes and Thoughts:

Question(s) of the Week: Do you freely worship God out of a heart of gratitude and praise, or do your personal preferences get in the way?

Answer:

The Power of 1°

Make a Joyful Noise!

Psalm 100:1

1 Make a joyful noise to the Lord, all the earth!

Notes and Thoughts:

Question(s) of the Week: Is your worship full of joy or is it just noise?

Answer:

The Power of 1°

Psalms 100:2-5

2 *Serve the Lord with gladness! Come into his presence with singing!*

3 *Know that the Lord, he is God! It is he who made us, and we are his; we are his people, and the sheep of his pasture.*

4 *Enter his gates with thanksgiving, and his courts with praise! Give thanks to him; bless his name!*

5 *For the Lord is good; his steadfast love endures forever, and his faithfulness to all generations.*

Notes and Thoughts:

Question(s) of the Week: Are you praising God throughout the week or only on Sundays? Are you bringing your individual praise into corporate worship?

Answer:

The Power of 1°

Mark 10:17-22

17 And as he [Jesus] was setting out on his journey, a man ran up and knelt before him and asked him, "Good Teacher, what must I do to inherit eternal life?"

18 And Jesus said to him, "Why do you call me good? No one is good except God alone.

19 You know the commandments: 'Do not murder, Do not commit adultery, Do not steal, Do not bear false witness, Do not defraud, Honor your father and mother.'"

20 And he said to him, "Teacher, all these I have kept from my youth."

21 And Jesus, looking at him, loved him, and said to him, "You lack one thing: go, sell all that you have and give to the poor, and you will have treasure in heaven; and come, follow me."

22 Disheartened by the saying, he went away sorrowful, for he had great possessions.

1 Samuel 16:7b

7b "For the Lord sees not as man sees: man looks on the outward appearance, but the Lord looks on the heart."

Notes and Thoughts:

Question(s) of the Week: What parts of your hidden life are full of sin and need to be addressed? How are you going to correct these areas that are holding you back from authentic worship?

Answer:

The Power of 1°

Exodus 2:11-14

11 One day, when Moses had grown up, he went out to his people and looked on their burdens, and he saw an Egyptian beating a Hebrew, one of his people.

12 He looked this way and that, and seeing no one, he struck down the Egyptian and hid him in the sand.

13 When he went out the next day, behold, two Hebrews were struggling together. And he said to the man in the wrong, "Why do you strike your companion?"

14 He answered, "Who made you a prince and a judge over us? Do you mean to kill me as you killed the Egyptian?" Then Moses was afraid, and thought, "Surely the thing is known."

Exodus 3 (Portions)

1 Now Moses was keeping the flock of his father-in-law, Jethro, the priest of Midian, and he led his flock to the west side of the wilderness and came to Horeb, the mountain of God.

2 And the angel of the Lord appeared to him in a flame of fire out of the midst of a bush. He looked, and behold, the bush was burning, yet it was not consumed.

4 When the Lord saw that he turned aside to see, God called to him out of the bush, "Moses, Moses!" And he said, "Here I am."

10 *"Come, I will send you to Pharaoh that you may bring my people, the children of Israel, out of Egypt."*

11 *But Moses said to God, "Who am I that I should go to Pharaoh and bring the children of Israel out of Egypt?"*

Notes and Thoughts:

Question(s) of the Week: *In what ways has God restored you from something, to ultimately plant you firmly where He wants you to be?*

Answer:

The Power of 1°

Proverbs 14:30

30 A tranquil heart gives life to the flesh, but envy makes the bones rot.

Ecclesiastes 4:4

4 Then I saw that all toil and all skill in work come from a man's envy of his neighbor. This also is vanity and a striving after wind.

Notes and Thoughts:

Question(s) of the Week: Who or what are you envious of?

Answer:

The Power of 1°

Be Still and Know God

Psalm 46:10a

10a "Be still, and know that I am God."

Notes and Thoughts:

Question(s) of the Week: *How are you doing in your personal life at being still and knowing He is God?*

Answer:

The Power of 1°

Colossians 3:23-24

23 Whatever you do, work heartily, as for the Lord and not for men,

24 knowing that from the Lord you will receive the inheritance as your reward. You are serving the Lord Christ.

Notes and Thoughts:

Question(s) of the Week: Are you working heartily for the Lord in everything you do?

Answer:

The Power of 1°

Luke 4:14-16

14 And Jesus returned in the power of the Spirit to Galilee, and a report about him went out through all the surrounding country.

15 And he taught in their synagogues, being glorified by all.

16 And he came to Nazareth, where he had been brought up. And as was his custom, he went to the synagogue on the Sabbath day, and he stood up to read.

Hebrews 10:24-25

24 And let us consider how to stir up one another to love and good works,

25 not neglecting to meet together, as is the habit of some, but encouraging one another, and all the more as you see the Day drawing near.

Notes and Thoughts:

Question(s) of the Week: When you think about your personal worship, is God pleased with your level of engagement? Are you "worshipping regularly" or simply "going through the motions" each week?

Answer:

The Power of 1°

Luke 10:38-42

38 Now as they went on their way, Jesus entered a village. And a woman named Martha welcomed him into her house.

39 And she had a sister called Mary, who sat at the Lord's feet and listened to his teaching.

40 But Martha was distracted with much serving. And she went up to him and said, "Lord, do you not care that my sister has left me to serve alone? Tell her then to help me."

41 But the Lord answered her, "Martha, Martha, you are anxious and troubled about many things,

42 but one thing is necessary. Mary has chosen the good portion, which will not be taken away from her."

<u>**Notes and Thoughts:**</u>

Question(s) of the Week: *How is your busy schedule distracting you from "sitting at Jesus' feet", listening to Him and worshipping Him?*

Answer:

The Power of 1°

Matthew 12:9-14

9 *He went on from there and entered their synagogue*

10 *And a man was there with a withered hand. And they asked him, "Is it lawful to heal on the Sabbath?" - so that they might accuse him.*

11 *He said to them,* "Which one of you who has a sheep, if it falls into a pit on the Sabbath, will not take hold of it and lift it out?

12 *Of how much more value is a man than a sheep! So it is lawful to do good on the Sabbath."*

13 *Then he said to the man,* "Stretch out your hand." *And the man stretched it out, and it was restored, healthy like the other.*

14 *But the Pharisees went out and conspired against him, how to destroy him.*

Notes and Thoughts:

Question(s) of the Week: *Have you become legalistic in any way? Are you more focused on following Christian rules or following God?*

Answer:

The Power of 1°

Mark 9:20-24

20 And they brought the boy to him. And when the spirit saw him, immediately it convulsed the boy, and he fell on the ground and rolled about, foaming at the mouth.

21 And Jesus asked his father, "How long has this been happening to him?" And he said, "From childhood.

22 And it has often cast him into fire and into water, to destroy him. But if you can do anything, have compassion on us and help us."

23 And Jesus said to him, "'If you can'! All things are possible for one who believes."

24 Immediately the father of the child cried out and said, "I believe; help my unbelief!"

<u>*Notes and Thoughts:*</u>

Question(s) of the Week: *What circumstances are you currently facing where your faith is being challenged? Have you asked God to increase your faith during these trials?*

Answer:

The Power of 1°

The Doubting Believer: Jesus' Response
Read: Mark 9:25-29

Mark 9:25-29

25 And when Jesus saw that a crowd came running together, he rebuked the unclean spirit, saying to it, *"You mute and deaf spirit, I command you, come out of him and never enter him again."*

26 And after crying out and convulsing him terribly, it came out, and the boy was like a corpse, so that most of them said, "He is dead."

27 But Jesus took him by the hand and lifted him up, and he arose.

28 And when he had entered the house, his disciples asked him privately, "Why could we not cast it out?"

29 And he said to them, *"This kind cannot be driven out by anything but prayer."*

Notes and Thoughts:

Question(s) of the Week: *Are you relying on your own strength and experiences in your Christian walk, or on God's divine power?*

Answer:

The Power of 1°

Luke 5:15-16

15 But now even more the report about him went abroad, and great crowds gathered to hear him and to be healed of their infirmities.

16 But he would withdraw to desolate places and pray.

Notes and Thoughts:

Question(s) of the Week: Do you 'carve' out time to spend with God or is He the greatest priority in your life?

Answer:

_____ *The Power of 1°*

John 2:13-16

13 The Passover of the Jews was at hand, and Jesus went up to Jerusalem.

14 In the temple he found those who were selling oxen and sheep and pigeons, and the money-changers sitting there.

15 And making a whip of cords, he drove them all out of the temple, with the sheep and oxen. And he poured out the coins of the money-changers and overturned their tables.

16 And he told those who sold the pigeons, "Take these things away; do not make my Father's house a house of trade."

<u>**Notes and Thoughts:**</u>

Question(s) of the Week: *Are there unholy activities occurring in our church that need to be addressed? How have we become complacent in our response to sinful activities around us?*

Answer:

The Power of 1°

Strength Under Control

Matthew 5:5

5 "Blessed are the meek, for they shall inherit the earth."

Notes and Thoughts:

Question(s) of the Week: *Are you living a life of meekness while tapping into the strength of Christ? Are you living under His control or your own?*

Answer:

The Power of 1°

1 Chronicles 16 (Portions)

23 Sing to the Lord, all the earth! Tell of his salvation from day to day.

24 Declare his glory among the nations, his marvelous works among all the peoples!

25 For great is the Lord, and greatly to be praised, and he is to be feared above all gods.

27 Splendor and majesty are before him; strength and joy are in his place.

28 Ascribe to the Lord, O families of the peoples, ascribe to the Lord glory and strength!

31 Let the heavens be glad, and let the earth rejoice, and let them say among the nations, "The Lord reigns!"

32 Let the sea roar, and all that fills it; let the field exult, and everything in it!

34 Oh give thanks to the Lord, for he is good; for his steadfast love endures forever!

36 "Blessed be the Lord, the God of Israel, from everlasting to everlasting!" Then all the people said, "Amen!" and praised the Lord.

Notes and Thoughts:

Question(s) of the Week: Do you declare God's glory in all you say and do? Do you give Him the freedom to move in your life at all times?

Answer:

The Power of 1°

Mark 10:42-45

42 And Jesus called them to him and said to them, "You know that those who are considered rulers of the Gentiles lord it over them, and their great ones exercise authority over them.

43 But it shall not be so among you. But whoever would be great among you must be your servant,

44 and whoever would be first among you must be slave of all.

45 For even the Son of Man came not to be served but to serve, and to give his life as a ransom for many."

Notes and Thoughts:

Question(s) of the Week: Are you a leader of servants or a servant leader? What are some examples of people being effective servant leaders in our worship ministry?

Answer:

The Power of 1°

2 Corinthians 10:5b

5b *Take every thought captive to obey Christ.*

Notes and Thoughts:

Question(s) of the Week: Do you control your thoughts or do your thoughts control you?

Answer:

The Power of 1°

Matthew 16:24

24 Then Jesus told his disciples, "If anyone would come after me, let him deny himself and take up his cross and follow me."

Notes and Thoughts:

Question(s) of the Week: In your life, where do you need to relinquish control to God?

Answer:

The Power of 1°

Major Over Minor is the Key

Matthew 23:23

23 *"Woe to you, scribes and Pharisees, hypocrites! For you tithe mint and dill and cumin, and have neglected the weightier matters of the law: justice and mercy and faithfulness. These you ought to have done, without neglecting the others."*

Notes and Thoughts:

Question(s) of the Week: *Are you majoring on the minor things and minoring on the major ones? Is your attention focused on Christ, or less significant matters?*

Answer:

The Power of 1°

2 Corinthians 12:7b-10

7b A thorn was given me in the flesh, a messenger of Satan to harass me, to keep me from becoming conceited.

8 Three times I pleaded with the Lord about this, that it should leave me.

9 But he said to me, *"My grace is sufficient for you, for my power is made perfect in weakness."* Therefore I will boast all the more gladly of my weaknesses, so that the power of Christ may rest upon me.

10 For the sake of Christ, then, I am content with weaknesses, insults, hardships, persecutions, and calamities. For when I am weak, then I am strong.

Notes and Thoughts:

Question(s) of the Week: Where are you letting your limitations keep you from giving God your best?

Answer:

The Power of 1°

God, an Old Man and a Young Lad

1 Samuel 3:4-10

4 Then the Lord called Samuel, and he said, "Here I am!"

5 and ran to Eli and said, "Here I am, for you called me." But he said, "I did not call; lie down again." So he went and lay down.

6 And the Lord called again, "Samuel!" and Samuel arose and went to Eli and said, "Here I am, for you called me." But he said, "I did not call, my son; lie down again."

7 Now Samuel did not yet know the Lord, and the word of the Lord had not yet been revealed to him.

8 And the Lord called Samuel again the third time. And he arose and went to Eli and said, "Here I am, for you called me." Then Eli perceived that the Lord was calling the boy.

9 Therefore Eli said to Samuel, "Go, lie down, and if he calls you, you shall say, 'Speak, Lord, for your servant hears.'" So Samuel went and lay down in his place.

10 And the Lord came and stood, calling as at other times, "Samuel! Samuel!" And Samuel said, "Speak, for your servant hears."

Notes and Thoughts:

Question(s) of the Week: Who do you go to first for advice and counsel: God, or other people?

Answer:

_____ *The Power of 1°*

Genesis 22:1-5

1 After these things God tested Abraham and said to him, "Abraham!" And he said, "Here I am."

2 He said, "Take your son, your only son Isaac, whom you love, and go to the land of Moriah, and offer him there as a burnt offering on one of the mountains of which I shall tell you."

3 So Abraham rose early in the morning, saddled his donkey, and took two of his young men with him, and his son Isaac. And he cut the wood for the burnt offering and arose and went to the place of which God had told him.

4 On the third day Abraham lifted up his eyes and saw the place from afar.

5 Then Abraham said to his young men, "Stay here with the donkey; I and the boy will go over there and worship and come again to you."

Notes and Thoughts:

Question(s) of the Week: *How is God asking you to step out in faith? Will you respond in immediate obedience as Abraham did?*

Answer:

_____ *The Power of 1°*

Genesis 22:6-13

6 And Abraham took the wood of the burnt offering and laid it on Isaac his son. And he took in his hand the fire and the knife. So they went both of them together.

7 And Isaac said to his father Abraham, "My father!" And he said, "Here I am, my son." He said, "Behold, the fire and the wood, but where is the lamb for a burnt offering?"

8 Abraham said, "God will provide for himself the lamb for a burnt offering, my son." So they went both of them together.

9 When they came to the place of which God had told him, Abraham built the altar there and laid the wood in order and bound Isaac his son and laid him on the altar, on top of the wood.

10 Then Abraham reached out his hand and took the knife to slaughter his son.

11 But the angel of the Lord called to him from heaven and said, "Abraham, Abraham!" And he said, "Here I am."

12 He said, "Do not lay your hand on the boy or do anything to him, for now I know that you fear God, seeing you have not withheld your son, your only son, from me."

13 And Abraham lifted up his eyes and looked, and behold, behind him was a ram, caught in a thicket by his horns. And Abraham went and took the ram and offered it up as a burnt offering instead of his son.

<u>**_Notes and Thoughts:_**</u>

Question(s) of the Week: _Are you willing to go to the ends of_
the earth to obey God?

Answer:

_____ **_The Power of 1°_**

The Vessel

Jeremiah 18:1-6

1 The word that came to Jeremiah from the Lord:

2 "Arise, and go down to the potter's house, and there I will let you hear my words."

3 So I went down to the potter's house, and there he was working at his wheel.

4 And the vessel he was making of clay was spoiled in the potter's hand, and he reworked it into another vessel, as it seemed good to the potter to do.

5 Then the word of the Lord came to me:

6 "O house of Israel, can I not do with you as this potter has done?" declares the Lord. "Behold, like the clay in the potter's hand, so are you in my hand, O house of Israel."

<u>**Notes and Thoughts:**</u>

Question(s) of the Week: *What areas are you resistant to the Potter molding you into what He wants you to become?*

Answer:

—————————————————————— *The Power of 1°*

Matthew 7:1-5

1 "Judge not, that you be not judged.

2 For with the judgment you pronounce you will be judged, and with the measure you use it will be measured to you.

3 Why do you see the speck that is in your brother's eye, but do not notice the log that is in your own eye?

4 Or how can you say to your brother, 'Let me take the speck out of your eye,' when there is the log in your own eye?

5 You hypocrite, first take the log out of your own eye, and then you will see clearly to take the speck out of your brother's eye."

Notes and Thoughts:

Question(s) of the Week: Do you thoroughly examine your own sinful life before judging other Christians?

Answer:

The Power of 1°

Proverbs 30:8-9

8 *Remove far from me falsehood and lying; give me neither poverty nor riches; feed me with the food that is needful for me,*

9 *lest I be full and deny you and say, "Who is the Lord?" or lest I be poor and steal and profane the name of my God.*

Luke 11:3

3 *"Give us each day our daily bread"*

<u>Notes and Thoughts:</u>

Question(s) of the Week: Are you content in God providing you with "daily bread" or do you have an insatiable appetite for more?

Answer:

The Power of 1°

David and the Ark: David's Six Paces

2 Samuel 6:13-15

13 And when those who bore the ark of the Lord had gone six steps, he sacrificed an ox and a fattened animal.

14 And David danced before the Lord with all his might. And David was wearing a linen ephod.

15 So David and all the house of Israel brought up the ark of the Lord with shouting and with the sound of the horn.

Notes and Thoughts:

Question(s) of the Week: When worshipping God, do you worship with all your might, or do you restrain yourself because of church norms and the perceptions of others?

Answer:

The Power of 1°

2 Samuel 6:20-22

20 And David returned to bless his household. But Michal the daughter of Saul came out to meet David and said, "How the king of Israel honored himself today, uncovering himself today before the eyes of his servants' female servants, as one of the vulgar fellows shamelessly uncovers himself!"

21 And David said to Michal, "It was before the Lord, who chose me above your father and above all his house, to appoint me as prince over Israel, the people of the Lord - and I will celebrate before the Lord.

22 I will make myself yet more contemptible than this, and I will be abased in your eyes. But by the female servants of whom you have spoken, by them I shall be held in honor."

Notes and Thoughts:

Question(s) of the Week: Do you focus more on pleasing God or pleasing people? In what specific ways?

Answer:

The Power of 1°

2 Samuel 7:7

7 'In all places where I have moved with all the people of Israel, did I speak a word with any of the judges of Israel, whom I commanded to shepherd my people Israel, saying, "Why have you not built me a house of cedar?"'

Notes and Thoughts:

Question(s) of the Week: What decision(s) have you made recently that you have not sought God's direction on yet? How are you going to address this?

Answer:

The Power of 1°

Ephesians 6:1

1 *Children, obey your parents in the Lord, for this is right.*

John 10:10b

10b *"I came that they may have life and have it abundantly."*

Notes and Thoughts:

Question(s) of the Week: *Where are you acting on your own accord and not listening to the Master's directions?*

Answer:

The Power of 1°

Luke 15 (Portions)

11 And he said, "There was a man who had two sons.

12 And the younger of them said to his father, 'Father, give me the share of property that is coming to me.' And he divided his property between them.

13 Not many days later, the younger son gathered all he had and took a journey into a far country, and there he squandered his property in reckless living.

14 And when he had spent everything, a severe famine arose in that country, and he began to be in need.

20 And he arose and came to his father. But while he was still a long way off, his father saw him and felt compassion, and ran and embraced him and kissed him.

21 And the son said to him, 'Father, I have sinned against heaven and before you. I am no longer worthy to be called your son.'

28 But he [the older brother] was angry and refused to go in. His father came out and entreated him,

29 but he answered his father, 'Look, these many years I have served you, and I never disobeyed your command, yet you never gave me a young goat, that I might celebrate with my friends.

30 But when this son of yours came, who has devoured your property with prostitutes, you killed the fattened calf for him!'

31 *And he said to him, 'Son, you are always with me, and all that is mine is yours.*

32 *It was fitting to celebrate and be glad, for this your brother was dead, and is alive; he was lost, and is found.'"*

<u>**Notes and Thoughts:**</u>

Question(s) of the Week: Where are you inflating your perception of yourself while deflating your perception of others? What steps will you take to more accurately see yourself and others from God's perspective?

Answer:

The Power of 1°

Know Nothing but Christ

1 Corinthians 2:2

2 For I decided to know nothing among you except Jesus Christ and him crucified.

John 17:3

3 *"And this is eternal life, that they know you the only true God, and Jesus Christ whom you have sent."*

Notes and Thoughts:

Question(s) of the Week: With Jesus Christ being the "object" of your worship, what has hindered your efforts to get to know Him better?

Answer:

The Power of 1°

Matthew 5:41

41 *"And if anyone forces you to go one mile, go with him two miles."*

Notes and Thoughts:

Question(s) of the Week: *Who is God bringing to your mind right now for you to walk the second mile with?*

Answer:

The Power of 1°

John 15:1-11

1 "I am the true vine, and my Father is the vinedresser.

2 Every branch in me that does not bear fruit he takes away, and every branch that does bear fruit he prunes, that it may bear more fruit.

3 Already you are clean because of the word that I have spoken to you.

4 Abide in me, and I in you. As the branch cannot bear fruit by itself, unless it abides in the vine, neither can you, unless you abide in me.

5 I am the vine; you are the branches. Whoever abides in me and I in him, he it is that bears much fruit, for apart from me you can do nothing.

6 If anyone does not abide in me he is thrown away like a branch and withers; and the branches are gathered, thrown into the fire, and burned.

7 If you abide in me, and my words abide in you, ask whatever you wish, and it will be done for you.

8 By this my Father is glorified, that you bear much fruit and so prove to be my disciples.

9 As the Father has loved me, so have I loved you. Abide in my love.

10 If you keep my commandments, you will abide in my love, just as I have kept my Father's commandments and abide in his love.

11 These things I have spoken to you, that my joy may be in you, and that your joy may be full."

Notes and Thoughts:

Question(s) of the Week: *What type of fruit are you producing? What is the Vinedresser pruning in your life?*

Answer:

_____ *The Power of 1°*

Matthew 6:19-21

19 *"Do not lay up for yourselves treasures on earth, where moth and rust destroy and where thieves break in and steal,*

20 *but lay up for yourselves treasures in heaven, where neither moth nor rust destroys and where thieves do not break in and steal.*

21 *For where your treasure is, there your heart will be also."*

<u>**Notes and Thoughts:**</u>

Question(s) of the Week: Which treasure chest are you depositing into the most?

Answer:

The Power of 1°

Mark 16:15

15 And he said to them, "Go into all the world and proclaim the gospel to the whole creation."

Romans 10:17

17 So faith comes from hearing, and hearing through the word of Christ.

Notes and Thoughts:

Question(s) of the Week: When is the last time you shared the good news of Christ with someone?

Answer:

The Power of 1°

Obedience vs. Sacrifice

1 Samuel 15:22

22 And Samuel said, "Has the Lord as great delight in burnt offerings and sacrifices, as in obeying the voice of the Lord? Behold, to obey is better than sacrifice, and to listen than the fat of rams."

Notes and Thoughts:

Question(s) of the Week: What is God convicting you of right now? How are you going to respond in obedience?

Answer:

The Power of 1°

John 3 (Portions)

26 And they came to John and said to him, "Rabbi, he who was with you across the Jordan, to whom you bore witness - look, he is baptizing, and all are going to him."

28 You yourselves bear me witness, that I said, 'I am not the Christ, but I have been sent before him.'

30 "He must increase, but I must decrease."

Notes and Thoughts:

Question(s) of the Week: Are you drawing attention to yourself rather than God? How can you reflect God more effectively to others?

Answer:

The Power of 1°

Scripture References by Week

Week 27 - *John 2:13-16*

Week 28 - *Matthew 5:5*

Week 29 - *1 Chronicles 16 (Portions)*

Week 30 - *Mark 10:42-45*

Week 31 - *2 Corinthians 10:5b*

Week 32 - *Matthew 16:24*

Week 33 - *Matthew 23:23*

Week 34 - *2 Corinthians 12:7b-10*

Week 35 - *1 Samuel 3:4-10*

Week 36 - *Genesis 22:1-5*

Week 37 - *Genesis 22:6-13*

Week 38 - *Jeremiah 18:1-6*

Week 39 - *Matthew 7:1-5*

Week 40 - *Proverbs 30:8-9, Luke 11:3*

Week 41 - *2 Samuel 6:13-15*

Week 42 - *2 Samuel 6:20-22*

Week 43 - *2 Samuel 7:7*

Week 44 - *Ephesians 6:1, John 10:10b*

Week 45 - *Luke 15 (Portions)*

Week 46 - *1 Corinthians 2:2, John 17:3*

Week 47 - *Matthew 5:41*

Week 48 - *John 15:1-11*

Week 49 - *Matthew 6:19-21*

Week 50 - *Mark 16:15, Romans 10:17*

Week 51 - *1 Samuel 15:22*

Week 52 - *John 3 (Portions)*

Notes

Made in the USA
Coppell, TX
09 December 2020